Clever Little Di

Story by Beverley Randell

Illustrations by Ben Spiby

Little Dinosaur
came out of his hole.

"I can't see Big Dinosaur today,"
he said.
"I will go for a walk.
I will go down to the river."

Little Dinosaur
liked eating dragonflies
down by the river.

A green dragonfly
came out of the forest.

Little Dinosaur ran after it.
He jumped up at it again and again.

Little Dinosaur jumped
on Big Dinosaur's tail.

Oh, no!

This made Big Dinosaur wake up!

Big Dinosaur got up.

He ran after Little Dinosaur.

"**Help!**" cried Little Dinosaur.

9

Little Dinosaur had to get away.
He ran into the forest.

"Big Dinosaur can't run fast
in the forest," he said.

Little Dinosaur ran very fast.

He ran and ran.

Big Dinosaur ran after Little Dinosaur.

But the trees got in his way.

Big Dinosaur had to go back.

And Little Dinosaur ran home!

Clever Little Dinosaur had got away!
He ran back to his hole
and jumped inside.